SO YOU THINK YOU KNOW HAIR, DO YOU?

A POP QUIZ

**Because hair is just a thing on our heads, we tend to think we know all about it.
But are you really a hair expert?**

Test your knowledge.

1. If you get scared enough, your hair will turn white overnight.
   True   False

2. If you get scared enough, your hair will stand straight up in the air on end.
   True   False

3. Cutting hair makes it grow back faster.
   True   False

4. Shaving hair makes it grow back thicker.
   True   False

5. Some dogs have naturally blue hair.
   True   False

6. If you eat the crusts on your bread, it will make your hair curly.
   True   False

7. There is such a thing as a werewolf.
   True   False

8. People shed more hair in the summer.
   True   False

9. Some people dye their hair red using actual cow urine.
   True   False

10. Tumors in the body sometimes grow hair.
    True   False

11. Marilyn Monroe was a natural blonde, and Elvis had naturally black hair.
    True   False

12. Each hair on your head is tied in a little knot at the end under your scalp, which is what keeps it attached.
    True   False

13. By examining one hair on your head, a scientist can tell what you had for dinner last Saturday night.
    True   False

14. If you never cut your hair, it will grow so long that it'll trail around behind you on the floor.
    True   False

How is it that a dog can have blue hair?

What does your hair say to a scientist?

What kind of tumor grows hair?

Stay tuned . . .

D1210810

Answers: 1. F, but almost true; 2. F, unless your hair is very, very short; 3. F; 4. F; 5. T; 6. F; 7. F, but kinda true; 8. T; 9. T (don't try this at home!); 10. T; 11. F and F; 12. F; 13. F; in most cases. 14. Very F in most cases.

Dolphin with a Ponytail?
Scientists believe that both dolphins and whales were once hairy creatures. The hair slowed them down in the water, so, over time, they lost all but a few tufts.

4

THE HAIRY BOOK

THE (UNCUT) TRUTH
ABOUT THE WEIRDNESS OF HAIR

BY THE EDITORS OF PLANET DEXTER

SCHOLASTIC INC.
New York Toronto London Auckland Sydney

PLANET DEXTER®

ILLUSTRATED BY JACK KEELY

ISBN 0-590-11532-4

Copyright © 1996 by The Editors of Planet Dexter.
Illustrations copyright © 1996 by Jack Keely.
All rights reserved. Published by Scholastic Inc., 555 Broadway, New York, NY 10012,
by arrangement with Addison-Wesley Publishing Company.

SCHOLASTIC and associated logos are trademarks and/or registered trademarks of Scholastic Inc.

12 11 10 9 8 7 6 5 4 3 2 1   7 8 9/9 0 1 2/0

Printed in the U.S.A.   08
First Scholastic printing, October 1997

And Now a Message from Our Corporate Lawyer:

"Neither the Publisher nor the Author shall be liable for any damage that may be caused or sustained as a result of conducting any of the activities in this book without specifically following instructions, conducting the activities without proper supervision, or ignoring the cautions contained in the book."

PLANET DEXTER®

LET'S START WITH YOU AND YOUR EX-MUSTACHE

Shocking but 100 percent true: You once had a mustache.

Really. Yes, you did. Even if you're a girl. And it gets worse.

You once had not only a mustache, but a completely hairy body – hair almost everywhere, even on your forehead. Only the palms of your hands and the soles of your feet were hairless. No offense, but you were about as hairy as an ape.

"No way!" you are saying.

"Why don't I remember this? How come there are no pictures of me looking so hairy?" Well, because it happened before you were born, when you were still floating around in your mom's mid-section. It happens to everyone.

About four months before a baby is born, fine and silky colorless hair called lanugo grows almost all over the baby's body. Picture it like the cornsilk strands that cover an ear of corn when you husk it. The lanugo grew first on your eyebrows and face, and around your mouth – a baby beard! Then it grew on the rest of your bod.

Finally, about a month before your birth, all the hair fell off.

So, actually, you've already had a mustache, and, you've already gone bald. Big-time baldness. It's a gigantic mystery why this happens. Does it mean that, in the way distant past, we used to be born with all that hair? Does the hair protect us, somehow, before birth? No one can say for certain. But the hair is there.

Hair is with us from the get-go.

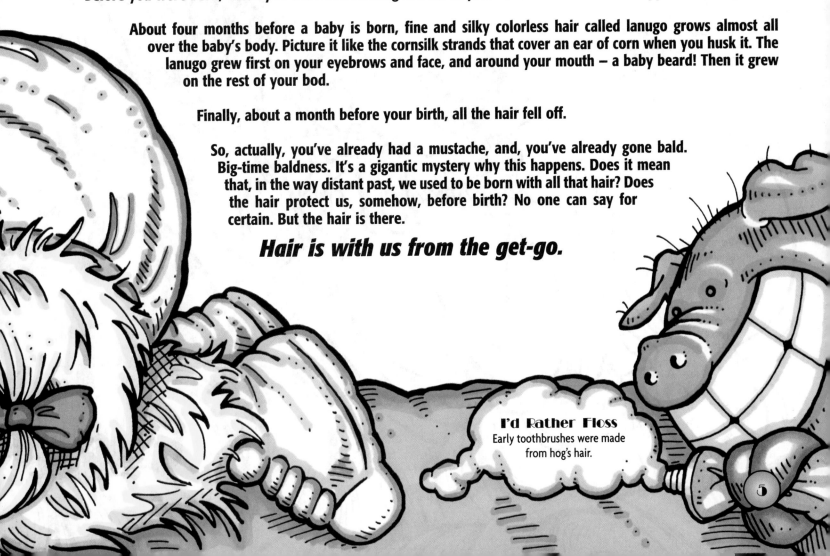

I'd Rather Floss
Early toothbrushes were made
from hog's hair.

Blonds have MORE hair

LIFE IS NOT FAIR

Unless you're hopelessly bad at counting, you know how many legs you have, how many arms and eyes. Counting hair, though, would be both pointless and a huge pain in the rump. Here's a secret: if you can answer the question, "What color is your hair?" you can also answer the question, "Roughly how many hairs are on your head?"

HAIR COLOR = *Number of Hairs on Head*
(APPROXIMATELY)

RED = **90,000 hairs on head**
BLACK = **108,000**
BROWN = **110,000**
BLOND = **140,000**

Busy, Busy
Right now, about 90 percent of your hair is growing, about 10 percent of it has stopped growing and is just resting before falling out. Each hair rests for about 100 days before it falls out.

Why do blond people get more hair?

No one is quite sure. It doesn't seem fair, but consider it this way.

Time a blond person would spend counting head hairs, if counting one each second and not taking a break until finished: 39 hours.

A huge pain in the rump, you'd have to agree.

But . . . Time a red-haired person would spend: 25 hours.

Still a huge pain in the rump!

So, either way, it's a lot of hair. And, actually, we all lose about 40 to 100 hairs a day — they just fall out normally, into our hair brushes, or onto the floor, or into whatever we're eating. So getting a good count would be extremely difficult.

Besides, the hair on our heads is only the tip of the iceberg . . .

Just a Little off the Top, Please

At one time, in addition to cutting hair, barbers pulled teeth, performed surgery, and put leeches on people in order to bleed them. The red and white on the barbers' pole stands for blood and bandages.

HAUNTED HAIR

YOU CAN'T RUN.
YOU CAN'T HIDE.
IT'S EVERYWHERE.

That colorful mass of hair is on your head — and not say, on your elbow — because it insulates and protects the brain, or so some scientists claim.

But if you think of hair as being only on the heads and bodies of people and cute, furry animals, think again. Bet you can't find the 13 examples of hair in this haunted parlor.

Find a complete list on the HairBrainer's Page at the end of this book.

FIVE THINGS TO BE GRATEFUL FOR
WHEN YOU'VE GOT A BAD CUT

1. Be grateful that your head isn't covered with fingernails or toenails instead of hair. Hair grows about six inches a year, but fingernails grow only about one inch a year, and toenails only about one-half to one inch a year.

Plus, a toenail head would be mighty unflattering.

2. Be grateful that you don't live in ancient Greece. There, people cut off their hair and gave it to the gods whenever something really good (like getting married), or something really bad (like a death of someone they liked) happened. Anyone who wanted long hair would have to hope for a boring life.

Long Enough
The world record for long hair is held by Mata Jagdamba, of India. Thirteen feet, ten and a half inches. If she wanted to, she could play jump rope with her own hair.

3. Be grateful that you're alive in this century. In the 16th and 17th centuries, there was at times such a tremendous demand for human hair (to make into wigs) that a stranger might sneak up behind you with a pair of scissors and help themselves to your mane. Young children had to be watched especially carefully, because they made easy targets.

10

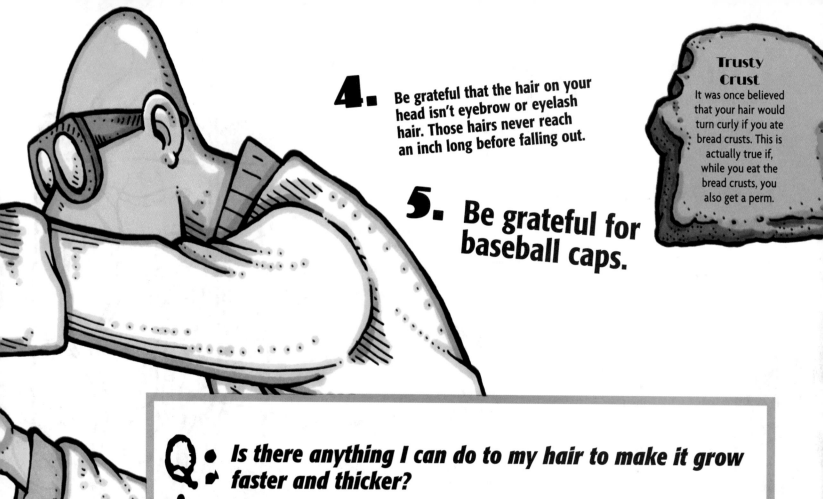

4. Be grateful that the hair on your head isn't eyebrow or eyelash hair. Those hairs never reach an inch long before falling out.

5. Be grateful for baseball caps.

Trusty Crust
It was once believed that your hair would turn curly if you ate bread crusts. This is actually true if, while you eat the bread crusts, you also get a perm.

Q: *Is there anything I can do to my hair to make it grow faster and thicker?*

A: *No.*
Some people think that shaving hair makes it grow back thicker. Or that cutting hair makes it grow faster. But the tiny part of the hair that's alive is stuck in the skin of your scalp and can't tell if you're cutting or shaving the dead part of the hair. It just keeps growing in its normal way, lah dee dee, lah dee dah, no matter what you do.

Q: *Is it true that if I rub my scalp, more hair will grow there?*

A: Alas, your head is not a lamp with a genie in it. Some people do indeed claim that rubbing the skin on your scalp causes more blood to circulate around the hair follicles, which helps them produce more hair. But your scalp has more blood in it than probably any other part of the body, with the exception of the kidney, so a little extra circulation from rubbing doesn't make a difference.

HAIR ANATOMY 101
JUST THE FACTS, MA'AM

Actual size of how far hair penetrates into head —

Hair shaft

Skin

Sebaceous gland that provides waterproof oil for hair and skin.

A Muscle attached to the hair can cause it to stand on end when you're cold or very scared, or emotionally touched by something. If you had really, really short hair, like the hair on your arms, you might be able to see the hair stand on end. But if it's any longer, it can't hold up the weight of the dead hair, so it looks like it's lying flat.

Bulb of follicle where new keratin, the hair protein material, is formed. As more keratin is made, it pushes upward into the hair shaft, causing the hair to grow. The shape of the bulb helps hold hair in the skin.

Follicle

Sweat gland

Cortex (where the keratin is)

Cuticle (tough outer shell)

Nerves so you can sense breeze and pulled hair.

Smooth City
In Carrizozo, New Mexico, it's illegal for women to go out in public if they haven't shaved their legs and, if necessary, their faces.

Follicle shape of a person with **curly hair**

Follicle shape of a person with **straight hair**

Follicle shape of a person with **wavy hair**

Hair Anatomy 202

STUFF WE TOTALLY MADE UP

FOR THOSE WHO REQUIRE MORE ENTERTAINMENT

Hair
is at this angle so that lice can use hair as a pole in lice pole-vaulting festivals.

Skin
viewed way too close up, so it looks like frosting on a cake.

Gland
that broadcasts jazz.

A Muscle
that allows hair to dance to jazz.

Gland
that supplies soft drinks to dancing hair.

Hair is tied
by the tiny rabbit in a triple knot to keep it in the head.

Nerves
so you can feel like upchucking before a big test.

Fly doo-doo —

A tiny rabbit lives in here
and lays little protein eggs, which she then jams up into the hair shaft, causing your hair to get longer.

Chewy rich nougat on the inside

Crunchy milk chocolate on the outside

Follicle shape of a person who eats lots of pinto beans

Follicle shape of a round person.

Follicle shape of a person who eats lots of jelly beans

The Neck Test
Some poets say they can tell a good poem if, when they hear it read, the hair on the back of their neck stands up.

13

SCARY AND ICKY HAIR

THE A-MAZE-ING STORY OF MEDUSA
THIS HAIR BITES, MAN

Medusa has a bad reputation. She's a mythological creature, a Gorgon, who, yeah, okay, has living snakes where other people have hair. And, all right, sure, she's got sharp fangs and a beard. And, yes, true, anyone who looks at her or at her bearded, snake-haired, sharp-fanged Gorgon sisters **Euryale** and **Sthenno** will instantly turn to stone.

But she started out as a nice person. A very pretty girl with only good hair days. The god **Neptune** admired her, and then attacked her in the temple of the goddess **Minerva**. Enraged, Minerva turned Medusa into a snake-head.

Sculptures of Gorgon heads have sometimes been placed on buildings or tombstones to keep away evil forces.

Here, Yowie Yowie Yowie
There have been more than 3,000 reportings of glimpses of the Yowie, a gorilla-like "great hairy man" creature said to live in the eastern mountain areas of Australia.

HAIRBALLS AND OTHER GAGGERS

SOME GROSS THINGS YOU MIGHT NOT WANT TO READ WHILE EATING

When you think "hairball," you probably think "cat." Cats swallow a lot of hair when they groom themselves, and then they can't digest the hair, so they hock up a bundle of their own wet fur.

You've probably never seen a human cough up a hairball (you'd remember, if you had), but people do indeed form hairballs sometimes, too. In humans, a hairball is called a **bezoar**.

Yank-ee Doodle

Trichotillomania is the word for a mental illness that causes people to want to pull out some of their own hair. A trichotillomaniac feels better once the hair is yanked out, and will sometimes pull out the hair of friends, family, or strangers. Or the hair of pets. Or dolls.

A bezoar in a human can be made all of hair, or of hair and something else, like food. Humans don't generally eat more than the occasional stray hair, but when they do, it's a very bad thing. One young woman who chewed on her hair a lot had to have an operation because she wasn't able to eat normally anymore. The surgeon who looked in her intestines found an eight-to-nine-inch bezoar there. Obviously, he removed it pronto and took a photo of it to show to friends.

Goats, antelopes, llamas, and other cud-chewing animals get bezoars, too, and apparently theirs are pleasant to look at. Kind of smooth and hard, like a marble. This type of bezoar was once considered very fashionable. Queen Elizabeth I of England is said to have owned a bezoar, and kept it in a gold frame.

Beyond Angel Hair Pasta
Trichophagia is the word for the practice of eating hair. Not a recommended thing to do.

17

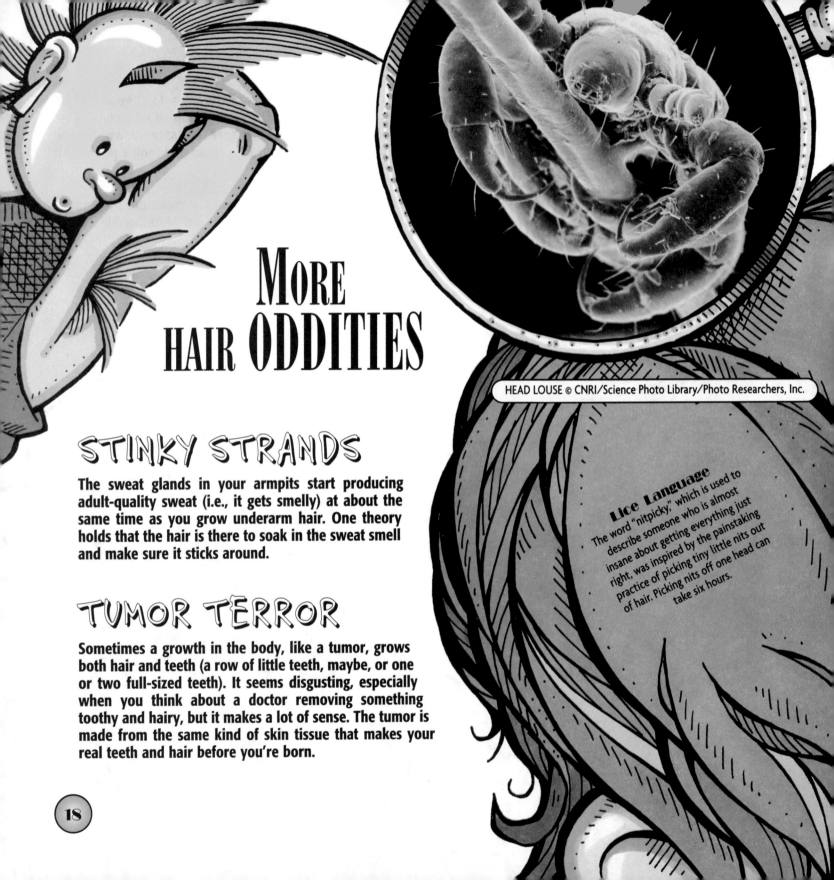

MORE HAIR ODDITIES

STINKY STRANDS

The sweat glands in your armpits start producing adult-quality sweat (i.e., it gets smelly) at about the same time as you grow underarm hair. One theory holds that the hair is there to soak in the sweat smell and make sure it sticks around.

TUMOR TERROR

Sometimes a growth in the body, like a tumor, grows both hair and teeth (a row of little teeth, maybe, or one or two full-sized teeth). It seems disgusting, especially when you think about a doctor removing something toothy and hairy, but it makes a lot of sense. The tumor is made from the same kind of skin tissue that makes your real teeth and hair before you're born.

Lice Language

The word "nitpicky," which is used to describe someone who is almost insane about getting everything just right, was inspired by the painstaking practice of picking tiny little nits out of hair. Picking nits off one head can take six hours.

18

LICE-A-RONI

Surprising Facts About The Hair Pests

- Lice, tiny greyish bugs with no wings, hang out in hair, but they don't eat hair. They suck blood from the scalp, and leave itchy lice spit under your skin.

  - Lice would be just as happy to infest the hair of adults, but they prefer kids because kids give them more access to other heads. Kids are always putting their heads together. Adults like to keep their heads way far away from other heads.

    - Lice would rather live on a clean scalp than a dirty one.

      - Lice live about 40 days, and in that time the female lice lay about 50 to 100 eggs, which are about the size of the period at the end of this sentence, or smaller. To get rid of head lice, you have to comb or pick all of those eggs (called nits) out of the hair.

        - Lice have a hard time crawling through thick hair, which is why they prefer thin-haired people.

          - Send lice flowers if you want them to leave: Some of the medications made to get rid of lice contain chyrsanthemum flower extracts.

Not So Smooth
Humans have about the same number of hair follicles that chimpanzees do.

HAIR AS A CLUE

WHAT A SCIENTIST OR DETECTIVE CAN TELL ABOUT YOU BY STUDYING YOUR HAIRS

Tree Magic
People once believed that if you had asthma (a breathing difficulty), you could cure it by cutting off a lock of your hair and putting that lock in a knot of a tree. When the tree's bark grew over the knot hole, hiding the hair, you were supposed to be cured.

At the scene of a crime, a person sometimes walks around with a piece of tape wrapped around his hand, sticking it to everything in sight.

What is that person doing? Gathering hairs!

Hairs are like the bread crumbs in "Hansel and Gretel." We drop them wherever we go, and a very careful detective, under the right conditions (like no wind, no vacuum cleaners), could track us just by following the trail of hair we leave behind.

A skilled "hair and fiber examiner" can tell a human hair from pet hair, and can even say whether the hair was dyed, whether it was pulled out of the head, or whether it just plain fell out.

Q: *If a scientist found one of my hairs lying around, what could she tell?*

A: The scientist could, first of all, tell if it was your hair. Each hair contains deoxyribonucleic acid, or DNA, and your DNA is like your fingerprint – no one else has one like it, unless you've got an identical twin.

Q: *Can the scientist tell what I have eaten?*

A: Well, sure – if the scientist is sitting with you while you eat it. But if the scientist is just checking out your hair with fancy equipment, all that shows up really well are signs that you have digested certain drugs or poisons. With some drugs, a hair can tell a scientist if you took them as long ago as three months back.

BALDNESS: LIFE'S BIG "HUH?"

When a guy goes bald, it's not that his hair just falls out. It's more that, for some unknown reason, the hair follicles in his head decide that instead of producing the hair he's always had, they'll produce very fine, colorless, almost invisible hair instead.

So a bald man's not really bald, he just has hair that's hard to see.

People who study the bod know that the male hormone androgen helps cause baldness. Men who have too much of it often get smaller hairs on their head, but also get hairier elsewhere — like on the shoulders, chest, or feet. The hair-making follicles don't move to the shoulders or chest or feet, but it seems as if they do, which is why you might call the change "Follicle Migration."

No one knows exactly why men go bald. Even if a doctor knows which people in a man's family have gone bald, and even if the doctor can measure the androgen in a man's body, there's no way (yet) to predict if the man will go bald.

Men in their 40s sometimes notice unexpected hair sticking out of their ears, too. It's the normal ear-hair, only it's turned into long, coarse hair. Magic.

Q: Why don't women lose their hair?

A: Sometimes they do, although they rarely go completely bald. Older women notice that their hair is thinner, and some of them lose hair in patches. Some women lose a bunch of hair after having a baby. But that hair usually grows back.

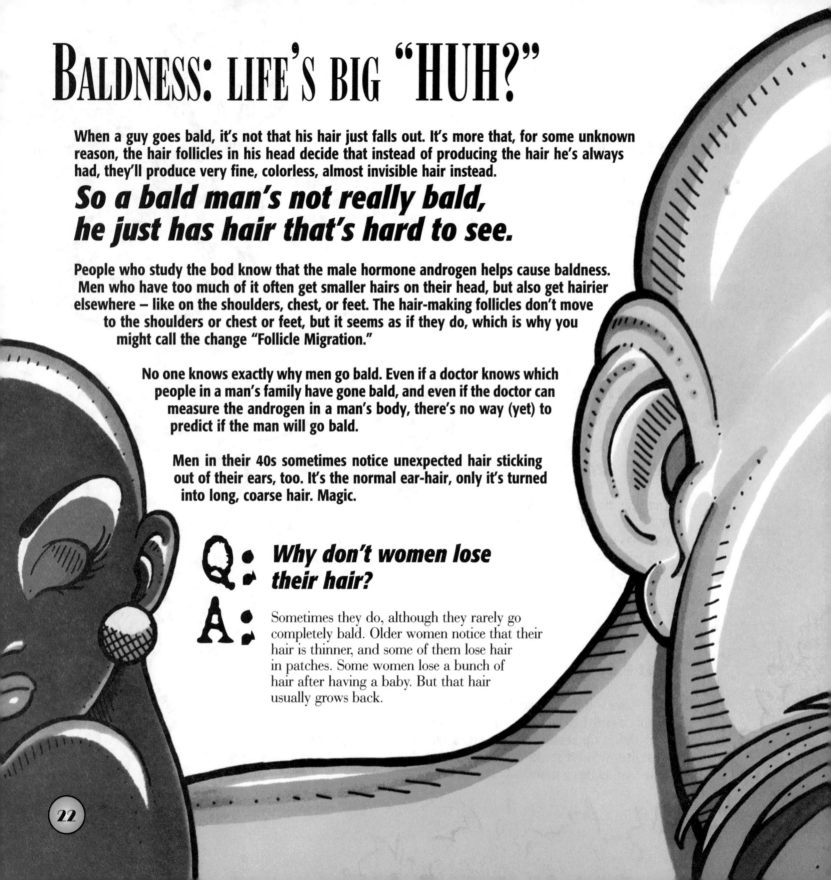

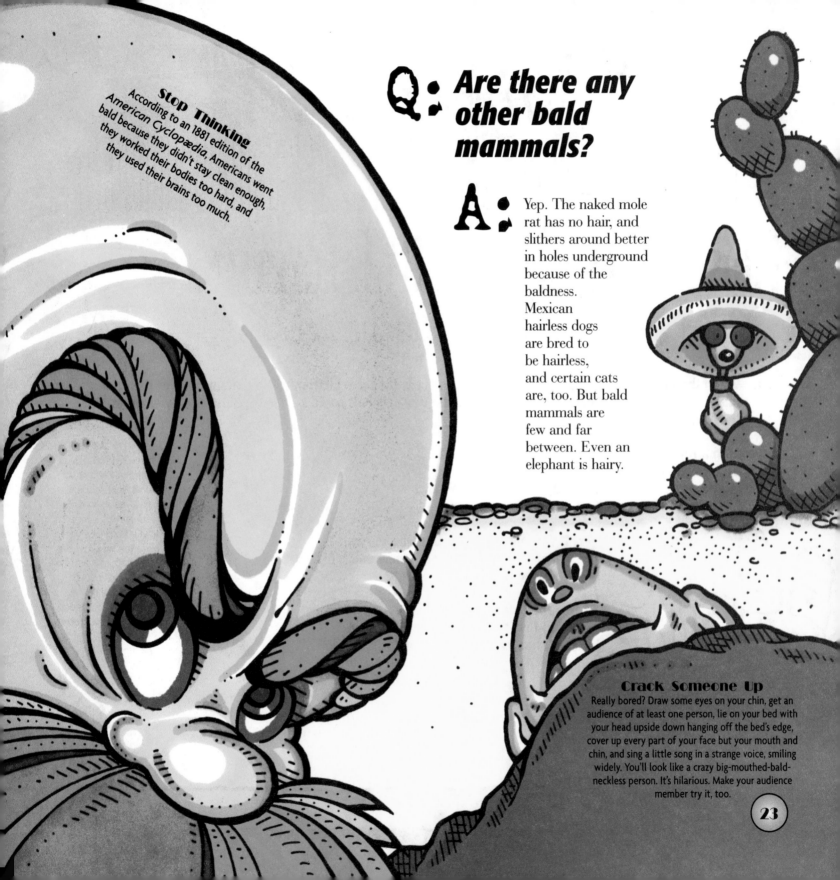

Q: Are there any other bald mammals?

A: Yep. The naked mole rat has no hair, and slithers around better in holes underground because of the baldness. Mexican hairless dogs are bred to be hairless, and certain cats are, too. But bald mammals are few and far between. Even an elephant is hairy.

23

THOSE WACKY, HAIR-FREE EGYPTIANS

ANOTHER MULTIPLE CHOICE ORDEAL

1. When the ancient Egyptians were preparing a mummy, they'd get nervous if they found one of the mummy's hairs lying around. They believed that a person's hair could be used against him by enemies. So they'd gather up the stray hair and place it_____.

   a) in a roaring fire
   b) in the mummy's tomb
   c) in a stone box, which they'd bury with a dead bird

2. Ancient Egyptians thought hair was _____ and _____, so they all, male and female, shaved it off and wore wigs.

   a) ugly and wicked
   b) foul-smelling and hard to clean
   c) hot and annoying

Real Drips
If you went to visit an ancient Egyptian at home, your host might give you a wax cone filled with sweet-smelling oils. You would place this on your head, the warmth of your head would melt the cone, and you'd enjoy the sweet-smelling oils dripping down your face.

3. If human hair or wool wasn't available for making the wigs, the ancient Egyptians would sometimes use_____.

a) grass
b) fur from a monkey's armpit
c) long beans strung together

4. Only the _____ ancient Egyptians had wigs made out of their own hair rather than the hair of other people or of sheep.

a) royal
b) popular
c) poorest

A First
Some people think wigs were first invented in ancient Egypt.

Answers: 1. b; 2. c; 3. a; 4. c

25

PIGS FOR WIGS

Not everyone was as cool about wigs as the ancient Egyptians were.

As tough as this is to imagine, there was a time in America, France, and England when almost all men and many women and quite a number of children wore wigs every day just because it was fashionable.

These wigs caused lots of trouble.

HORRID BUSHES

In 1675, the Massachusetts Court announced that men who wore wigs looked too much like women. Puritan minister Increase Mather, around the same time, called wigs *"horrid bushes of vanity."*

Hair Removal

The phrase "keep your wig on" came to mean "calm down" because in the 1700s men who were about to have a fistfight would take their wigs off, to keep them clean.

MAC AND CHEESE

In 1773, some foolish-looking guys started wearing wigs that stuck up in the air about a foot and a half above the head. They'd often place a tiny hat on top of the hair lump. These wigs were called Macaroni wigs. When Yankee Doodle "Stuck a feather in his cap and called it Macaroni," he was imitating the men wearing Macaroni wigs.

METALLICA

Some wigs around 1750 were made of iron or copper wire.

WIG SWIPERS

In 18th-century London, wig stealers would walk through crowds carrying baskets on their shoulders. Inside the baskets were sometimes little boys who would grab the wigs off unsuspecting people on the street, then disappear back into the basket.

Yo, Fathead

The term "big wig," meaning an important person, comes from a time, in the 17th Century, when you could tell what a person did for a living by the size of his wig. People in well-paying professions wore, yup, big wigs.

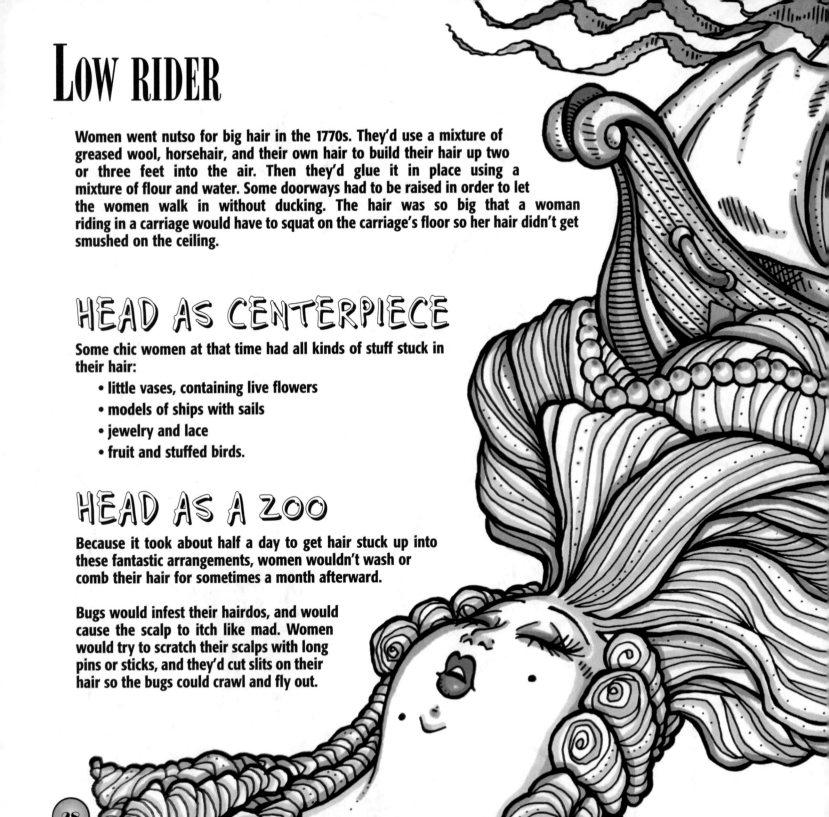

Low Rider

Women went nutso for big hair in the 1770s. They'd use a mixture of greased wool, horsehair, and their own hair to build their hair up two or three feet into the air. Then they'd glue it in place using a mixture of flour and water. Some doorways had to be raised in order to let the women walk in without ducking. The hair was so big that a woman riding in a carriage would have to squat on the carriage's floor so her hair didn't get smushed on the ceiling.

HEAD AS CENTERPIECE

Some chic women at that time had all kinds of stuff stuck in their hair:

- little vases, containing live flowers
- models of ships with sails
- jewelry and lace
- fruit and stuffed birds.

HEAD AS A ZOO

Because it took about half a day to get hair stuck up into these fantastic arrangements, women wouldn't wash or comb their hair for sometimes a month afterward.

Bugs would infest their hairdos, and would cause the scalp to itch like mad. Women would try to scratch their scalps with long pins or sticks, and they'd cut slits on their hair so the bugs could crawl and fly out.

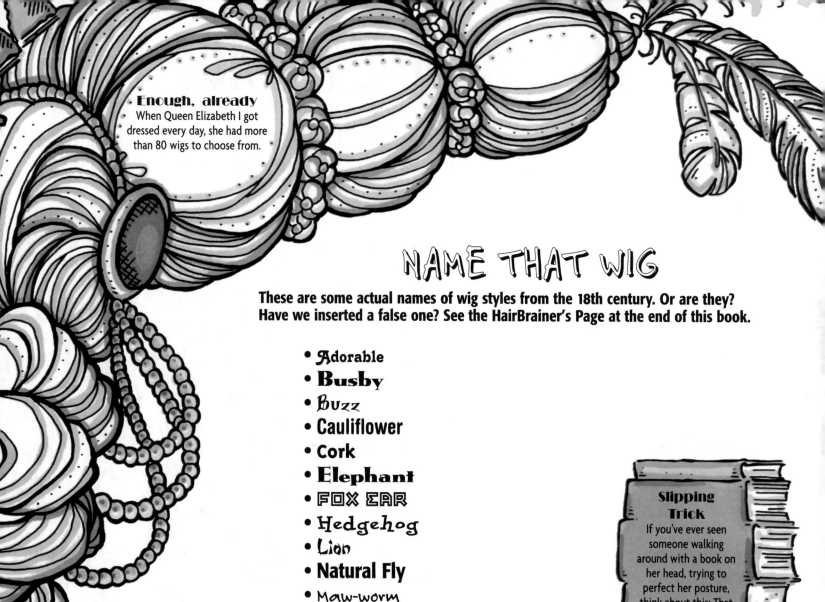

Enough, already
When Queen Elizabeth I got dressed every day, she had more than 80 wigs to choose from.

NAME THAT WIG

These are some actual names of wig styles from the 18th century. Or are they? Have we inserted a false one? See the HairBrainer's Page at the end of this book.

- Adorable
- **Busby**
- Buzz
- **Cauliflower**
- **Cork**
- **Elephant**
- FOX EAR
- Hedgehog
- Lion
- **Natural Fly**
- Maw-worm
- **Maitre d'hotel**
- Mousetrap
- Pigeon's wing
- **Prudence Puff**
- **Rhinoceros**
- **Rose Bag**
- Scratch
- She-dragon
- Staircase

Slipping Trick
If you've ever seen someone walking around with a book on her head, trying to perfect her posture, think about this: That exercise was invented in order to try to teach girls in Victorian times to keep their heads straight so their wigs wouldn't fall off.

29

P. 8, 9

1. Chilean Rose-Hair Tarantulas grow pinkish hairs and do not, as some tarantulas do, shoot hairs out of their bellies when irritated.

2. In olden days, Americans sometimes gathered up hairs from family members, and wove those hairs into a wreath.

3. The quills of a porcupine are hairs.

4. Some hairbrushes are made from the bristles (hairs) of a boar.

5. In Colonial America, people wove the hair of recently deceased loved ones into rings and broaches, and then wore the jewelry to remind them of that person.

6. Flies taste things by using the hairs on their legs.

7. This cat is coughing up hair he couldn't digest. He swallowed it when licking himself clean.

8. This is an old paintbrush made of hairs from a squirrel's tail; most new brushes are made of fake hair.

9. Some hoop skirts around the time of the American Civil War were made with a special kind of fabric stiffened with horse hair.

10. It was once considered very romantic to carry a lock of your beloved's hair in your locket.

11. Old plaster walls were made with real hair in them, to hold the plaster together.

12. The bow for a violin, viola, cello, or bass fiddle is strung with long white hairs gathered from a horse's tail.

13. The horn of a rhino is really just a lot of hairs fused together.

P. 28, 29

"Mousetrap" is the only one we made up, and it's not even the weirdest one.

FOUR REASONS TO GIVE YOUR HAIR

A ROUND OF APPLAUSE

Even Though It Can't Bow or Wave To Thank You Back Unless You Happen To Be Standing In a Strangely Blowing Wind

1. Without hair, all kinds of debris – dustballs, dirt, insects – would fly up your nose. That's because your nostrils contain hair that filters out the debris. Thank you, hair.

2. Without hair, your nose would run constantly. There are itsy-bitsy hairs in the nasal cavity that sweep snot back into your throat so you can swallow it away (see Planet Dexter's disgusting book, *Grossology: The Science of Really Gross Things!* for more gruesome details). When the hairs don't sweep – like when you have a cold – all the snot flows forward, out your nose, instead of back, down your throat. Thank you, thank you, hair!

3. Without hair, you couldn't hear. Microscopic hairs in the ears (you'll never see them) tickle nerves that allow us to make sense of sound vibrations. Gee, thank you, hair!

4. Without hair, you'd be a lot chillier than you are. Notice how, when you get goosebumps, your hair stands on end. That's because your body is trying to get the hair to trap air near your skin, and then warm the trapped air up, so you can wear it like a coat – an invisible coat of air. It doesn't usually make much difference on your arms. But the hair on your head does trap air and keep you warmer, since most of the body's heat tries to escape from your head. You rule, hair!

You said it, Jane
"I can't prove it, but I genuinely think I did coin the phrase 'bad hair day.'"

—Newswoman Jane Pauley, who says one of her hairdos was once described as looking like she had a dead squirrel on her shoulder.

Thanks!
(cue wild applause)